Contents

Introduction

Animals communicate in many different ways. They use sound, sight and chemicals to pass on information about themselves or their surroundings.

Sound and vision

Many animals communicate with sound. Social animals, such as meerkats and monkeys, use calls to warn group members of dangers. Tigers and lions roar to warn rivals to stay away from their **territories**. Birds and whales sing to attract a mate.

Animals also use **visual** signals to communicate. Chimpanzees use facial expressions to show excitement and fear. Dogs pull back their ears and bare their teeth when they feel threatened. Colour can be another important signal. The bright colours of poison dart frogs tell **predators** that they are poisonous. But bright colours can also be attractive. Male birds often have colourful feathers to attract females.

ANIMAL SCIENTISTS

Amazing Animal Communicators

by Leon Gray

Raintree is an imprint of Capstone Global Library Limited, a company incorporated in England and Wales having its registered office at 7 Pilgrim Street, London EC4V 6LB
Registered company number 6695582

www.raintree.co.uk
myorders@raintree.co.uk

ISBN: 978-1-4747-0216-4 (HB)
ISBN: 978-1-4747-0222-5

For Brown Bear Books Ltd:
Text: Leon Gray
Editor: Tim Harris
Picture Researcher: Clare Newman
Designer: Karen Perry
Design Manager: Keith Davis
Production Director: Alastair Gourlay
Editorial Director: Lindsey Lowe
Children's Publisher: Anne O'Daly

British Library Cataloguing in Publication Data
A full catalogue record for this book is available from the British Library.

Acknowledgements
Front cover: istock/Thinkstock
1, Piotr Gatlik/Shutterstock; 4, Wendy Dennis/FLPA; 5t, Tratong/Shutterstock; 5bl, Beboy/Shutterstock; 5br, Jason Prince/Shutterstock; 6, Kjersti Joergensen/Shutterstock; 6-7, David Osborn/Shutterstock; 7tl, Steve Russell Smith Photos/Shutterstock; 7tr, Peter Betts/Shutterstock; 8, Joost Van Uffelen/Shutterstock; 9t, Basel 01658/Shutterstock; 9b, Pierre I/Shutterstock; 10, M V Photo/Shutterstock; 11t, Ondreicka/Dreamstime; 11b, Andrea J Smith/Shutterstock; 12, Irina Ivanova/Shutterstock; 13l, Beboy/Shutterstock; 13r, Jez Bennett/Shutterstock; 14, iStock/Thinkstock; 14-15, Menno Schaefer/Shutterstock; 15tl, Amee Cross/Shutterstock; 15tr, Lightpoet/Shutterstock; 16, iStock/Thinkstock; 17t, Ulrich Baumgarten/Getty Images; 17b, HTU/Shutterstock; 18, Audrey Snider-Bell/Shutterstock; 19t, Robert Hamilton/Alamy; 19b, Steve Byland/Shutterstock; 20, Arto Hakola/Shutterstock; 21t, Brian Scott/Alamy; 21b, Shawn Hempel/Shutterstock; 22, Johan Swanepoel/Shutterstock; 22-23, Andrey Pavlov/Shutterstock; 23bl, Tim Harris; 23br, Fabio Maddei/iStock/Thinkstock; 24, Jez Bennett/Shutterstock; 25t, Jason Prince/Shutterstock; 25b, Stuart G. Porter/Shutterstock; 26, Cathy Keifer/Shutterstock; 27t, Matt Jeppson/Shutterstock; 27b, iStock/Thinkstock; 28, Paul Sawer/FLPA; 29t, Lukas Blazek/Dreamstime; 29b, Denis and Yulia Pogostins/Shutterstock.
t=top, c=centre, b=bottom, l=left, r=right

Some words are shown in bold, **like this**. You can find out what they mean by looking at the glossary.

Printed in China
20 19 18 17 16
10 9 8 7 6 5 4 3 2 1

Chemical messages

Some animals use chemicals to communicate. Many insects use chemicals called **pheromones** to signal to each other. Moths use these chemicals to attract mates. Bees release them when their hive is under attack. Other animals leave chemical signs as warnings. Wolves and big cats, such as lions and tigers, spray urine on trees. The odour warns rivals to stay away.

COPYCAT

Elephants use infrasound
to communicate with
each othe
use infras
volcanoes
erupts it
infrasour
ground. S
special in
listen for

WOW

A lion's roar can be heard from 8 kilometres (5 miles) away. Lions need to be heard far away because they defend big territories. The largest are 16 kilometres (10 miles) across.

Guide for readers

Throughout this book, special feature boxes accompany the main text, captioned photographs and illustrations. COPYCAT boxes highlight some of the ways in which people have been inspired by the animal world. WOW boxes provide incredible facts and figures about different animals.

Sound

Animals make lots of different sounds to communicate with one another. They call to attract their mates. Some animals sound alarms to warn that dangerous predators are nearby.

Attraction and alarm

Male alligators roar and splash in water to attract females. Many male birds sing to tell females that they are looking for a mate.

Many animals use sound as a danger signal. Dogs bark and growl to defend their territory from other dogs. Vervet monkeys have different calls for different predators. One sound warns that a python is nearby. The monkeys make a different sound when they spot a leopard.

Sperm whales communicate by sound when they swim underwater.

WHALES AND DOLPHINS CASE STUDY: PAGE 8

Animal language

Scientists think that some animals have a language in the same way that people do. Whales and dolphins make clicks and whistles. They use different noises to identify themselves, find food, attract mates and find their way about in the ocean.

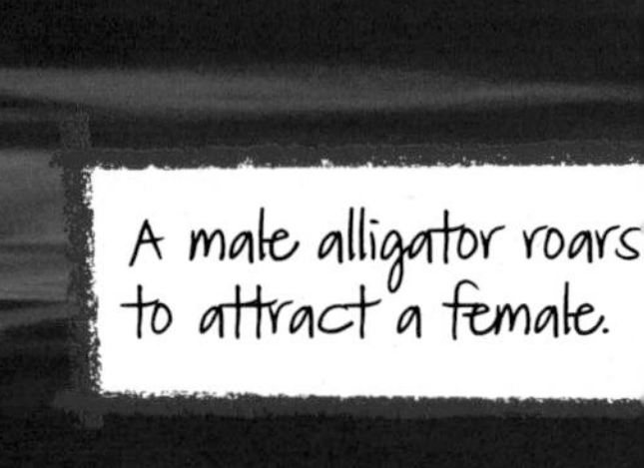

A male alligator roars to attract a female.

Male woodpeckers tap on wood to warn off rivals.
BIRDS CASE STUDY: PAGE 10
Elephants make low-pitched noises that travel long distances.
ELEPHANTS CASE STUDY: PAGE 12

Whales and dolphins

Whales belong to a group of mammals called cetaceans. Dolphins and porpoises are also in this group. Most cetaceans live in the ocean, though a few swim in rivers. All these creatures rely on sound to communicate in the water.

Humpback whales make sounds or tunes that may last for a few seconds or several hours.

Buzzes, clicks and whistles

Some whales and dolphins have teeth. These toothed whales use buzzes, clicks and whistles to communicate with each other. They make these sounds with special **organs** inside the head. The animals have a pair of **phonic lips** at the front of the nose. These vibrate to make sounds. There is a fatty organ called a melon inside the animal's forehead. This sends the sounds through the water. The sounds travel in waves.

Whale songs

Whales such as the blue whale are **filter feeders**. These whales have a voice box, or larynx, like people do. The voice box vibrates to make different sounds.

The humpback whale is a filter feeder. It is famous for the tuneful calls it makes. A humpback whale's song can last for more than five hours. The sound travels for hundreds of kilometres through the ocean. Male humpback whales sing to attract females during the mating season. The mating songs may also warn off other males.

COPYCAT

Whales and dolphins use sound to **navigate** in the ocean. They listen for the echoes of their calls. The echoes bounce off objects to build a "sound picture". People use a similar method, called sonar, to navigate in ships. Sonar is read on displays like this.

These striped dolphins whistle and click to each other to keep in touch.

Birds

Birds use different sounds to communicate. Woodpeckers send messages to each other by tapping their beaks against tree trunks. Warblers sing rich, tuneful songs.

Drumming birds

Woodpeckers are small or medium-sized birds that live in trees. They dig holes in tree trunks for their nests. They eat bugs that live beneath the bark. Woodpeckers communicate with each other by tapping their beaks on hard surfaces. They usually drum on trees or hollow logs. Sometimes they tap on the sides of houses.

Different woodpeckers drum with different patterns and **rhythms**. Some are very loud and can be heard from kilometres away. Woodpeckers drum most often in the breeding season. The sounds attract mates and tell rival woodpeckers to stay away.

Male and female woodpeckers communicate by drumming on trees.

A male warbler sings to tell any nearby females that it is ready to breed.

Singing warblers

Warblers communicate in a different way. They are small birds that live in forests, gardens and wetlands. Some warblers have bright feathers, but most are dull in colour. They make up for their drab appearance with their beautiful songs. The birds are hidden away in trees, and singing is a good way to communicate. Male warblers do most of the singing. Their songs show that the warblers are healthy and ready to breed. The loud melody attracts females and warns other males to stay away.

WOW

Woodpeckers tap hard against trees up to 10,000 times a day, so the birds need protection. A thick skull protects the bird's brain from the repeated bashing. The beaks of these birds are tough to shield them from the impact.

Elephants

Elephants are good communicators. They pass on information to other members of their group through touch and body language. They use sound to communicate with elephants further away.

Elephants wrap their trunks around each other as a sign of affection.

Trunk, ears and tail

An elephant's trunk is an important tool for communication. Lifting the trunk can signal anger or fear. Elephants also use their trunk to touch and to smell. The ears and tail also help elephants show their emotions. The animals flap the ears and raise the tail as a sign of excitement.

Sound is another way that elephants communicate. They have a very good sense of hearing and use a wide range of calls. Different sounds attract mates, warn of danger and keep the herd together. Female elephants grunt and growl to speak to their babies.

lephants use special sounds alled **infrasound** to ommunicate over long istances. The sounds are o low for humans to hear. lephants can hear them from everal kilometres away. They ake these sounds to find lephants that have wandered way from the herd. The ephants call again and again ntil they find the lost elephant. he animals then greet each ther with rumbling noises.

Elephants make loud trumpeting noises when they feel threatened.

COPYCAT

Elephants use infrasound to communicate with each other. Scientists use infrasound to study volcanoes. When a volcano erupts it sends waves of infrasound through the ground. Scientists use special instruments to listen for the waves.

Signals

Signals can attract other animals or warn them to stay away. An animal's colour and body shape is one kind of signal. It is called a badge. Some animals use another kind of signal. They behave in special ways to show affection, anger or fear.

Animal badges

The antlers of a male deer, or stag, are a signal of his age and power. If a stag has large antlers, other male deer stay away from him. Female deer are more likely to mate with him, though. The colourful feathers of a male bird show that he is healthy and would make a good mate.

Badges can also act as a warning. **Venomous** snakes often have colourful or stripy scales to signal that they are dangerous. Ladybirds have bright colours to show that they taste bad. These badges prevent predators from eating them.

A firefly signals it is ready to mate using a flashing light in its body.

FIREFLIES CASE STUDY: PAGE 16

Showing off

Many mammals, birds, reptiles and **invertebrates** perform displays to signal that they are ready to mate. Other displays act as a warning to stay away. Male wolves snarl at each other.

A rattlesnake coils itself and rattles its tail when it is threatened.

RATTLESNAKES CASE STUDY: PAGE 18

A male peafowl spreads its colourful tail to display to a female.

PEAFOWL CASE STUDY: PAGE 20

The large antlers on this red deer signal that it is fully grown and strong.

Fireflies

Fireflies are often called lightning bugs – and for a good reason. At night these insects light up the darkness with a dazzling display of flashing colours. Fireflies glow in the dark to communicate with each other.

A firefly's light comes from the last section of its body.

Hungry insects

There are about 2,000 diferent kinds of fireflies. They live in many **habitats**, including forests and wetlands. Adult fireflies mate in the spring. The female lays her eggs in the ground, and they hatch about four weeks later. The **larvae** that hatch out spend most of the summer feeding. When autumn comes, the larvae **hibernate**. They wake up the following spring and continue to eat for a few weeks. Then they are ready to change into adult fireflies.

ody glow

reflies glow because of a chemical action inside their bodies. An adult efly produces light signals at night. light flashes on and off. Male eflies attract females, and females tract males.

ome female fireflies use their lights to **re** males of another **species**. Instead mating with the males, the females it them.

COPYCAT

Forensic scientists use the same chemicals found inside the bodies of fireflies to uncover traces of blood at crime scenes.

Thousands of fireflies light up the forest with a yellowish-green glow.

Rattlesnakes

Rattlesnakes live in North and South America. These venomous reptiles are named for the rattle at the end of their tail. If a rattlesnake is threatened, it shakes the rattle as a warning signal.

Strong muscles in the snake's tail shake its warning rattle.

Snake life

Rattlesnakes are **cold-blooded** animals. They need to lie in sunshine to get warm. When they are not sunning themselves, they hide under rocks and wood so they can **ambush** prey.

Rattlesnakes hunt birds, small mammals and other reptiles. These deadly snakes have large fangs. They bite their prey to deliver a dose of **venom**. The venom acts quickly. Even if the prey escapes, the snake will track its scent and find the dead or dying animal. Then the snake swallows its victim whole.

Stay away

Despite their venomous bite, rattlesnakes have many predators. Badgers, birds of prey, owls and weasels hunt rattlesnakes. When they are threatened, rattlesnakes shake the rattle at the end of their tail. The rattle is made up of **modified** scales. They are hollow and lock together to form the rattle. The segments in the rattle knock against each other to make the rattling noise, warning predators to stay away.

WOW

Baby rattlesnakes, like the one below, do not have a rattle. Like all snakes, they shed their skin and grow a new one as they grow older. An extra segment is added to the rattle each time the snake sheds its skin.

A rattlesnake kills its prey with venom from two fangs in its upper jaw.

Peafowl

Peafowl are large, noisy birds. The males are called peacocks, and the females are peahens. Peacocks are famous for their colourful feathers. When a peacock wants to attract a peahen, he spreads his long tail feathers into a shimmering fan.

Beautiful birds

Indian peafowl live in forests in South Asia. They eat flowers, fruits, insects, small reptiles and frogs.

Male and female peafowl look very different. Peacocks have long, shimmering blue or green tail feathers. Peahens are usually dull grey, brown or green. They do not have long tail feathers like the males. Both males and females have a crest of feathers on their head.

A peacock calls loudly to attract a peahen.

Beautiful tail

A peacock's tail has about 200 feathers, and many of them have a brilliant eyespot. Each feather is 1.2 metres (4 feet) long. The male peafowl uses his beautiful feathers to find a mate.

WOW

A peacock has a dangerous defensive weapon. It uses sharp claws on its feet to stamp on snakes and other predators.

When a female comes close, the male turns his back on her and raises his tail feathers. Then he suddenly turns around to face her. He fans out his feathers and shakes them to show off the shimmering colours and eyespots. Female birds are attracted to the males with the longest feathers, brightest colours and the most eyespots.

A peacock spreads his tail into a beautiful fan.

Chemicals

Many animals communicate with invisible signals. They use scent to identify themselves, mark a territory or locate sources of food. Others use chemicals called pheromones to send messages.

Scent markers

All the ants in a **colony** have the same smell. If they meet an ant that smells different, they will attack it. Ants also lay trails of scent to food sources. Other ants follow the trails to find the food.

Some animals use scent to mark the boundaries of their territory. Antelope have glands on their faces. Big cats, such as tigers, have them under their tails. The animals rub the glands against trees and other plants to show that the territory belongs to them.

Skunks use a smelly scent to defend themselves. If an enemy comes too close, a skunk will spray it with a jet of horrible-smelling liquid.

Other animals send messages in the form of pheromones. Moths release pheromones that attract a mate from kilometres away. Other animals send out pheromones to signal danger.

Male lions defend territories that may cover many square kilometres of grassland.

LIONS CASE STUDY: PAGE 24

Ants can identify each other by their odour.

A skunk raises its tail to warn a predator. Only if this fails will the skunk spray foul-smelling liquid at its enemy.

SKUNKS CASE STUDY: PAGE 28

If a male moth senses the chemical signals given off by a female, the male will fly to her.

MOTHS CASE STUDY: PAGE 26

Lions

Lions live together in groups called prides. All the lions in a pride communicate with each other using sound and facial expressions. Male lions mark the edge of their territory with scent signals.

This male is marking the borders of his territory with scent.

Making friends and enemies

A lion's roar is a terrifying sound. Lions roar during arguments with other members of the pride. They also roar to warn off lions from outside. Lions growl, snarl, hiss, grunt and purr to signal that they are feeling content, angry or playful. They also nuzzle, rub and lick each other to show their feelings.

Lions have expressive faces. That helps them check on the mood of other members of the pride.

Chemical markers

The borders of a pride's territory may be many kilometres long. This makes it difficult to defend. Male lions warn visiting lions to keep out by leaving scent signals, just as tomcats do. The lions spray strong-smelling urine onto trees, bushes and rocks to mark their territory. They sniff any scent marks left by other lions. This way, lions from different prides can work out where their rivals are – and avoid fights that could be deadly.

WOW

A lion's roar can be heard from 8 kilometres (5 miles) away. Lions need to be heard far away because they defend big territories. The largest are 16 kilometres (10 miles) across.

Members of a lion pride roam around their territory in search of prey.

Moths

Scientists think that there are about 160,000 species of moths. They live all around the world. Adult moths use pheromones to communicate with each other.

The male moth's feather-shaped antennae detect pheromones sent out by a female.

Growing up

Moths start life as eggs. Tiny caterpillars hatch from the eggs and spend most of their time feeding. They grow quickly and shed their skin several times. When a caterpillar is ready to become an adult moth, it wraps itself up in a silk case called a cocoon. Inside the cocoon, the body of the caterpillar breaks down, and an adult moth develops. Eventually, a fully grown moth comes out of the cocoon.

This male silk moth has eyespots on its wings to confuse birds that might want to eat it.

Moths are nocturnal insects. They hide during the day and are active at night. They rely on pheromones to communicate in the darkness.

When a female moth is ready to mate she releases pheromones. Male moths sense the pheromones with the large, feathery antennae on their head.

A male moth can sense a single pheromone **molecule** from more than 10 kilometres (6 miles) away. He flies towards the scent and uses his antennae to home in on the female.

COPYCAT

Many scientists think that humans produce pheromones to attract each other. These pheromones are released by the underarms.

Skunks

Skunks live mainly in North and South America. Their bold patterns warn predators to keep away, but sometimes this warning is not enough. When a skunk is threatened, it sprays a jet of foul-smelling chemicals at its attacker.

A skunk's life

Most of the time, skunks live in burrows. They dig using their short, muscular legs and sharp front claws. In winter skunks stay in their burrows for several weeks to escape the cold. Skunks **forage** for food at dawn and dusk. They eat worms, frogs, small reptiles and mammals, berries and nuts.

Skunks are about the same size as house cats.

Chemical defence

A skunk has an excellent defence against predators. It sprays an oily liquid from two glands under its tail. The liquid has chemicals that smell so bad even large bears are driven away by it. A skunk can spray the liquid 3 metres (10 feet).

If the liquid gets into a predator's eyes, the predator may not be able to see for several days.

A skunk usually only sprays as a last resort. It will first stamp its feet, hiss and raise its tail as a warning. Most predators pay attention to the warning and leave skunks alone. A female skunk with her babies (called kits) does not give a warning. She will spray at the first sign of danger to protect her offspring.

COPYCAT

People add the same chemicals that skunks spray to supplies of natural gas. The foul smell acts as a warning in case there are fuel leaks.

Glossary

ambush surprise attack by a predator lying in wait for its prey

cold-blooded animal whose body temperature varies with that of its environment

colony group of animals, such as ants, that live together

filter feeders animals that eat by filtering tiny food particles from water

forage search for food

habitats natural homes of animals or plants

hibernate pass the winter in deep sleep

infrasound very low-pitched sound that humans cannot hear

invertebrates animals without backbones, such as insects

larvae maggot-like forms of young insects

lure attract and catch prey

modified something that has changed over a long period of time, such as part of an animal's body

molecule tiny particle that is too small to see. Everything is made up of molecules.

navigate direct a course over or through the ocean

organ part of an animal's body with a particular function

pheromones chemical signals made by animals

phonic lips structure in a whale's head that makes vibrations when air passes through it

predators animals that hunt and eat other animals

rhythms patterns of sound

species group of animals that share features, and can mate and produce young together

territory area of land that an animal defends from animals of the same kind

venom poisonous liquid made by predators, such as snakes, to disable prey

visual things that can be seen

Read more

Amazing Animal Communicators (Animal Superpowers), John Townsend (Raintree, 2012).

Bats (Animal Abilities), Charlotte Guillain (Raintree, 2013).

Elephants (Animal Families), Daniel Gilpin (Wayland, 2014).

Internet sites

BBC Nature
These webpages look at communication among baboons, chimpanzees, dolphins and crows.
www.bbc.co.uk/nature/adaptations/Animal_language

Communication in Animals
A Young People's Trust for the Environment factsheet.
ypte.org.uk/factsheets/communication-in-animals/scent

Natural History Museum
Information on the life of bats, including how they communicate.
www.nhm.ac.uk/nature-online/life/mammals/bats/session3

Index